Changing care and welfare

Britain before the Welfare State: a painting by Sir Luke Fildes shows homeless people queuing to get into a workhouse in London in 1874.

In every society there are people who are poor. Some are people who cannot survive without help: widows or orphans, people who are disabled or ill, and people who do not have work. Others may be poor through lack of opportunity, lack of ability or effort, or perhaps through bad luck.

Every society has its own views about how to care for the helpless and the poor. In Britain 100 years ago much less care was available than there is today. Few people expected the government or local authorities to provide any more than the bare minimum needed to stop the poor from starving. They expected charities rather than the government to care for them.

These attitudes began to change in the early years of this century. The Liberal government of 1906–1914 introduced new laws to help children, old people, the ill, and the unemployed. Later governments added to these measures in the Twenties and Thirties. Between 1945–1951 the Labour government introduced such a wide range of new measures that people described Britain as a 'Welfare State'.

This book describes how Britain became a Welfare State in the twentieth century. It asks why governments started to involve themselves in the care and welfare of people and their families. It shows how that involvement grew during the first half of the century and it examines some of the consequences.

Source 1

This picture appeared at the front of William Booth's book *Darkest England and the Way Out*, 1890.

1 Rich and poor in the 1900s

Source 1 is taken from a book written in 1890 by William Booth, leader of the Salvation Army. It shows, in Booth's words, 'the appalling extent of the misery and poverty existing in Great Britain.... In the raging sea, surrounding the Salvation lighthouse, are to be seen the victims of vice and poverty'. The scenes above the sea show how the Salvation Army tried to help the poor.

Poverty had existed throughout the nineteenth century. Groups such as the Salvation Army did what they could to help the poor but poverty was still widespread when the twentieth century began. In the early 1900s the view began to spread that helping the poor shouldn't be left only to volunteers. Instead the government should do more to help. In section 2 you will find out why this view gained ground. First let us look at the problem of poverty as people saw it at the start of this century.

A divided society

In 1905 a wealthy Member of Parliament published a book called *Riches and Poverty*. On the first page of the book he put the diagram opposite (Source 2).

It was only one of many books published in the 1900s on the subject of poverty and wealth. Dozens of books like it showed that British society was deeply divided between the poor and the rich.

Source 3 is taken from one of those books. It was by an American writer, Jack London, who spent the summer of 1902 living rough in the East End of London, posing as an out-of-work seaman. He wanted to find out how the poor in London lived. In this extract he describes walking along a crowded street with two other out-of-work men, looking for a place to sleep for the night.

Source 2

BRITISH INCOMES IN 1904

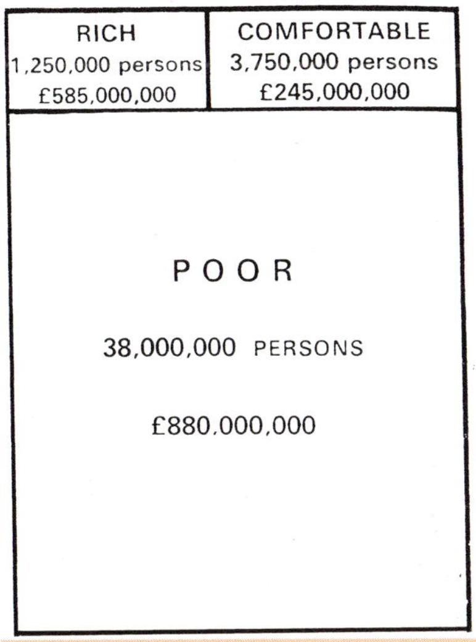

'British incomes in 1904'. This diagram appeared in *Riches and Poverty* by L.G. Chiozza Money, a Liberal Member of Parliament, in 1904.

Source 3

Jack London, *The People of the Abyss*, 1903. Note how he used italic type to emphasise his description.

Both kept their eyes on the pavement as they walked and talked, and every now and then one or the other would stoop and pick something up .... I thought it was cigar and cigarette stumps they were collecting, and for some time took no notice. Then I did notice.

From the slimy, spittle-drenched sidewalk, they were picking up bits of orange peel, apple skin, and grape stems, and they were eating them .... They picked up stray crumbs of bread the size of peas, apple cores so black and dirty one would not take them to be apple cores, and these things these two men took into their mouths, and chewed them, and swallowed them; and this, between six and seven o'clock in the evening of 20 August, year of our Lord 1902, in the heart of the greatest, wealthiest and most powerful empire the world has ever seen.

Poverty didn't exist only in London. In 1901 Seebohm Rowntree, son of the famous chocolate maker, published a survey on poverty in York. One of his findings was that four out of every ten wage-earners had to spend everything they earned on the bare necessities of life. All their wages, which averaged eighteen to 21 shillings (90p to £1.05), went on food, rent, clothing and fuel. In Source 4 he described what such people could not afford to buy.

Source 4

B. Seebohm Rowntree, *Poverty, A Study of Town Life*, 1901.

(They) must never spend a penny on railway fare or omnibus. They must never go into the country unless they walk. They must never purchase a halfpenny newspaper or spend a penny to buy a ticket for a popular concert .... They cannot save, nor can they join a sick club or Trade Union, because they cannot pay the necessary subscriptions. The children must have no pocket money for dolls, marbles or sweets. The father must smoke no tobacco, and must drink no beer. The mother must never buy any pretty clothes for herself or for her children .... Finally, the wage earner must never be absent from his work for a single day.

If any of these conditions are broken, the extra expenditure involved is met, and can only be met, by limiting the diet.

Rowntree included in his book many examples of the diet of poor people in York. Source 5 helps us to understand what he was saying. It is a list of the meals eaten in a week by the family of a carter earning twenty shillings (£1) a week.

Source 5

B. Seebohm Rowntree, *Poverty, A Study in Town Life*, 1901.

	Breakfast	**Dinner**	**Tea**	**Supper**
Friday	Bread, butter, tea	Bread, butter, toast, tea	Bread, butter, tea	
Saturday	Bread, bacon, coffee	Bacon, potatoes, pudding, tea	Bread, butter, shortcake, tea	Tea, bread, kippers
Sunday	Bread, butter, shortcake, coffee	Pork, onions, potatoes, Yorkshire pudding	Bread, butter, shortcake, tea	Bread and meat
Monday	Bread, bacon, butter, tea	Pork, potatoes, pudding, tea	Bread, butter, tea	One cup of tea
Tuesday	Bread, bacon, butter, coffee	Pork, bread, tea	Bread, butter, boiled eggs, tea	Bread, bacon butter, tea
Wednesday	Bread, bacon, butter, tea	Bacon, eggs, potatoes, bread, tea	Bread, butter, tea	
Thursday	Bread, butter, coffee	Bread, bacon, tea	Bread, butter, tea	

Writers like Rowntree and London drew attention to the terrible poverty that existed in parts of Britain. There were also writers who described another Britain inhabited by rich people. In a book published in 1909 a young aristocrat compared the lifestyles of poor people with those of some of his acquaintances. Source 6 is one of the comparisons he made.

Source 6

Arthur Ponsonby, *The Camel and the Needle's Eye*, 1909.

A single meal:

Bread	1d
Cheese	1d
1/4 lb of meat	3d
Potatoes and onions	2d
Jam	1d
1/2 pint of beer	2d
Total	10d*

Another meal:

Cantaloup Glacé	(Chilled melon)
Tortue Claire	(Turtle soup)
or Bisque Nantua	(Seafood soup)
Truites Saumonées Michigan	(Salmon-trout)
Mousse de Jambon a l'Escurial	(Ham pate)
Selle d'Agneau Montefiore	(Saddle of lamb)
Poularde Strasbourgeoise	(Chicken)
Salade Indienne	(Rice salad)
Cailles flanqués d'Ortolans	(Quails and buntings)
Asperges Verts. Sauce Mousseuse	(Asparagus. Sauce)
Pêches Framboisines	(Peaches in raspberry liqueur)
Friandises	(Sweets)
Fanchonettes Suisses	(Cream and meringue gateaux)

Hock, Claret, Port, Coffee and Liqueurs.

This dinner for twenty people cost £60, or £3* a head, without wine ...

10d (roughly 4p) in 1909 was worth about £1.40 in 1994 prices.
£3 was worth about £105 in 1994 prices.

Rich and poor not only ate very different meals but also lived in very different homes. Arthur Ponsonby reported that:

Source 7

Arthur Ponsonby, *The Camel and the Needle's Eye*, 1909.

In a house consisting of living-room, bedroom, and a small scullery live father, mother, three sons, also three children under ten and two men lodgers. Seven sleep in the bedroom ... and five sleep in the living-room; the only window of the latter room will not open ....

The landlord and lord of the manor of this district lives with his wife and family in a house containing over one hundred rooms, and is attended by a staff of 44 indoor servants. He has the choice of three other country residences and a town house, and owns over 186,000 acres.

People's housing and living conditions were being recorded in the 1900s not only by writers like Rowntree, London and Ponsonby, but also by local councils. Source 8 is a photograph taken by Liverpool City Council of a courtyard of houses in the city.

Source 8

Houses in Liverpool, photographed by the city council in 1906. The water pump in the courtyard was the only water supply for all the houses.

Questions

1 Look at Source 1. What does the writing on the pillars and on the sea tell you about (i) the causes, and (ii) the effects of poverty in Britain at the end of the nineteenth century?

2 **a** Look at Source 2. Use a calculator to find the average earnings in 1904 of (i) a 'poor' person, (ii) a 'comfortable' person, and (iii) a 'rich' person. (Divide the £ shown in each box by the number of persons shown in each box.)

b £1 in 1904 bought roughly the same as £35 today. Find the present day values of these average earnings by multiplying them by 35.

3 Read Source 3 again. Why might reading this description have made people think that something should be done to help the poor in London?

4 In source 4, Rowntree said that the only way a poor family could afford things like bus fares, toys, newspapers, beer, was to limit their diets.

a On what occasions might a family want to buy such things?

b Read the diet in Source 5. What part of it do you think the family could have limited in order to afford such things?

5 Arthur Ponsonby (Sources 6 and 7) was a wealthy man. Why do you think he recorded these comparisons between the diet and housing of rich and poor people?

2 Thinking about the poor

Books like Seebohm Rowntree's *Poverty* made a strong impression on many readers. Poverty became a leading subject for discussion among the ruling class. Newspapers and magazines frequently ran stories and features on the subject.

Why this sudden interest in poverty? There had been poverty in Britain for hundreds of years. Why did it become a major issue in the 1900s and not before? The sources in this section should help you to find three answers to that question.

Why did poverty become an issue in the 1900s?

One of the many people who read Rowntree's book was a 27-year-old Member of Parliament, Winston Churchill He wrote:

Source 1

Winston Churchill, letter written on 23 December 1901 to a Conservative Party politician in Birmingham.

I have lately been reading a book by Mr Rowntree called *Poverty* which has impressed me very much. It is quite evident ... that the American labourer is a stronger, larger, healthier, better fed and consequently more efficient animal than a large proportion of our population, and this is surely a fact which our unbridled Imperialists (keen suppporters of the British Empire) ...should not lose sight of. For my part, I can see little glory in an Empire which can rule the waves, and is unable to flush the sewers.

Rowntree's *Poverty* was published at a time when Britain was at war. Since 1899 the British army had been fighting the rebel Boers in South Africa. It took the British three years to win this war against much smaller, untrained forces. In 1902 the army had to turn down two out of every three men who volunteered to fight in the war, because they were unfit. Fears grew among the ruling class that the British people were being weakened by 'race degeneration' brought about by poverty. To investigate these fears, the government set up a Committee on Physical Deterioration in 1904. This recommended the introduction of medical inspections and free school meals in schools run by local authorities.

The following year, in 1905, the government set up a more general enquiry into the subject of poverty. Source 2 gives the conclusions of the enquiry, which lasted five years and covered the entire country.

Source 2

Adapted from the report of the Royal Commission on the *Poor Laws and Relief of Distress*, 1905–9.

Our investigations prove the existence in our midst of a class whose condition and environment is a peril to the whole community ....

No country, however rich, can permanently hold its own in the race of international competition, if hampered by an increasing load of this dead weight; or can successfully run an overseas empire if its own folk at home are sinking below the civilisation of its subject races abroad.

Views about how to deal with the problem of poverty differed widely. Some were harsh and unforgiving. One writer who was horrified by the poor health of army recruits, demanded that:

Source 3

Adapted from Arnold White, *Efficiency and Empire*, 1901.

We must abandon the idea that ... every poor man in need of help is an innocent victim .... A sterner attitude by the average man towards paupers is essential if England is to begin to deal with her unfit. Consider the army of 26,000 tramps who infest the high roads of England .... Get rid of them by locking them up for life .... Until we are content to see the idle perish ... little change for the better in the health of the people can be looked for.

The sight of poverty could also provoke great sympathy. A young man in Oxford at the turn of the century describes in Source 4 how the sight of poverty made him join the Labour Party.

Source 4

Interview with the son of a bricklayer's labourer, in Paul Thompson, *The Edwardians*, 1975, a book based on 444 interviews with old people remembering their youth in the 1900s.

I'll tell you what made me turn a Socialist .... I've seen boys when I went to school, I've seen one or two boys before they went into school at nine o'clock go round this back yard ... and the people who lived in the back, if they had some stale bread, they'd chuck the stale bread in pieces to the birds out on to the grass, you see. Two of the boys used to come out early, pick up that bread and eat it, cause they'd got nothing to eat to go to school. When I realised that, I thought to myself, well, England is supposed to be – it was – the most powerful and richest country in the world, and yet – nothing could be done. Why not? I tried to be a Socialist, and have been ever since.

Socialists in Britain came together in 1900 to form the Labour Party. They aimed to get better working conditions and greater equality of wealth for working people. Some members of the Liberal Party feared that the new Labour Party would take support away from themselves. In 1905, a leading member of the Liberal Party, David Lloyd George, spoke about what they must do to avoid losing support:

Source 5

David Lloyd George, speech on *Liberalism and the Labour Party*, 11 October 1906.

If at the end of an average term of office it were found that a Liberal Parliament had done nothing to cope seriously with the social condition of the people, to remove the national degradation of slums and widespread poverty and destitution in a land glittering with wealth ... then would a cry arise for a new party.

Over the next ten years, David Lloyd George was to take a leading part in social reform. However, it wasn't simply fear of losing support to the Labour Party that made him do this. Source 6 shows another, deeper motive for wanting to help the poor.

Source 6

David Lloyd George, speech on *Social Reform*, 1 October 1908.

I have had ... letters ... from people whose cases I have investigated – honest workmen thrown out of work, tramping the streets ... begging for work as they would for charity, and at the end of the day trudging home, disheartened and empty-handed, to be greeted by faces, and some of them little faces, haggard and pinched with starvation and anxiety. The day will come, and it is not far distant, that this country will shudder at its toleration of that state of things when it was rolling in wealth. I say again, that apart from its inhumanity and its essential injustice, it is robbery, it is confiscation of what is the workman's share of the riches of the land.

Source 7

David Lloyd George (left) and Winston Churchill (right) in 1908. Lloyd George was Chancellor of the Exchequer and Churchill was President of the Board of Trade.

Questions

1. Read Sources 5 and 6. If the Labour Party had not been formed, do you think Lloyd George would have wanted to help the poor? Explain your answer.
2. The sources in this section show several kinds of reasons for helping the poor. One reason is to do with the British economy. One is to do with politics. Another is to do with social justice and yet another with race. Which sources show each kind of reason?

3 The Liberal reforms of 1906–1914

In 1906 the Liberal Party won a landslide victory in the general election. There were now 400 Liberals in Parliament, compared with 157 Conservatives. There were also 83 Irish Nationalists and 30 Labour MPs, who all supported the Liberals. This huge majority gave an opportunity to Liberals like David Lloyd George and Winston Churchill to introduce daring new laws on social reform. This section describes those reforms and asks whether, as many people said, they led to a revolution in care.

The shadow of the workhouse: care before 1906

Before 1906 the only state-run social service was 'poor relief'. Using tests laid down by the Poor Law of 1834, Poor Law guardians could give tiny cash payments called 'outdoor relief' to people who were destitute through ill health, disablement, or old age. Those who did not pass the test, for example able-bodied unemployed people, could only get indoor relief – in a workhouse.

The workhouse was a kind of prison where poor people who had nowhere else to go lived under military discipline in return for basic meals and a bed. The poor hated and feared the workhouse, old people especially. Couples who had been married all their adult lives risked ending their days sleeping in separate dormitories and eating in silent, uniformed ranks. Source 1 gives an idea of why the workhouse was so hated.

Source 1

A meal time at the workhouse in Marylebone, London, in 1900.

Moving away from the Poor Law

The reforms which the Liberals introduced went far beyond the provisions of the Poor Law:

Children

- **Free school meals (1906)**. Free school meals for poor children could now be paid for out of local council rates. This meant that parents did not have to ask the Poor Law guardians for help.

• **School medical service (1907)**. Doctors went to schools to give children medical tests and to recommend treatment where needed.

• **The Children's Act (1908)** made it a legal offence for parents to neglect their children. Also, children could no longer be sent to prison under the age of fourteen. Instead, young offenders could be sent to Borstal, a kind of prison school named after the village where the first one opened.

• **School clinics (1912)**. Many families could not afford a visit to the doctor when the School Medical Service recommended treatment. In 1912 the government therefore opened school clinics where children could be treated.

The elderly

• **The Pensions Act of 1908** said that men and women over 70 were entitled to a weekly pension paid out of government funds. The pension was tiny – five shillings (25p) a week for a single person and 7s 6d ($37^1/_2$ p) for couples – about £8 and £12 in today's prices. Moreover, you could only draw the pension if you earned less than £26 a year (for single people; £39 for couples). However, small though it was, the pension came from government funds and people did not have to undergo a Poor Law test.

Workers

• **Labour Exchanges**. Unemployment pay was paid through a network of Labour Exchanges, set up in 1910 by Winston Churchill, President of the Board of Trade. As well as giving out unemployment pay, they provided information about job vacancies, so that workers looking for jobs no longer had to walk from one factory to the next looking for work.

• **The National Insurance Act (1911)** set up a National Insurance scheme. All workers in manual jobs or low-paid white-collar jobs had to join it. Each week they paid fourpence for insurance stamps to stick on a card. The employer added threepence and the government twopence. In return, an ill worker got sick pay of 10 shillings a week for 26 weeks as well as free medical treatment. This was provided by doctors who belonged to a 'panel' in each district. Doctors received a fee from the insurance fund for each 'panel' patient they treated.

• **The second part of the National Insurance Act**. This came into force in 1912. It gave unemployment insurance to $2^1/_4$ million workers in jobs liable to heavy seasonal unemployment, for example, building work. The workers, employers and the government each paid for $2^1/_2$ pence worth of insurance stamps a week. In return, an unemployed worker could receive seven shillings a week for a maximum of fifteen weeks in any one year.

The People's Budget

The Conservatives bitterly opposed many of these measures. This led to a major crisis over the way the country was governed. The crisis began in 1909 when the Chancellor, David Lloyd George, produced a budget to pay for the National Insurance scheme (see above).

The budget is a statement which the Chancellor makes to Parliament each year. In it, the Chancellor describes how the government will raise money to pay for its spending plans for the coming year. Lloyd George's budget was designed to raise £16 million for spending on insurance. This would be done by increasing income tax for the rich, by taxing profits on the sale of land, and by putting new taxes on petrol, cars, alcohol and tobacco.

The Conservatives in Parliament hated these proposals. They especially hated the tax on land, for many of them were landowners. Although they were in a minority in the House of Commons, they had a majority in the House of Lords. At that time, bills had to be approved by both Houses before they could become law. The Lords refused to pass the budget.

Parliament in crisis

For two centuries decisions about taxation had always been made by the Commons, with the Lords giving approval without question. The Liberal government said that the budget was therefore not a matter for the Lords to decide. They called an election to ask the people for their views. When the Liberals won this election, the Lords backed down and voted for the budget.

The government now decided that the Lords' powers must be reduced. It drew up a Parliament Bill saying that the Lords could have no say in money matters and could block other laws for no more than two years. Not surprisingly, the Lords refused to agree to this. After long arguments with the Lords, the Prime Minister decided on drastic action. He asked the king to add 500 Liberals to the House of Lords, giving the Liberals a majority there. When the king agreed, the Lords saw that they had lost and voted for the bill. It became the Parliament Act of 1911.

Reform or revolution?

At the time and since, people have disagreed about the importance of the Liberal reforms of 1906–14. Some see these reforms as a major break with the past which laid the foundations of the Welfare State. Flora Thompson, a Post Office worker in 1908, gave out some of the first old age pensions ever issued. She later wrote in her autobiography about what pensions meant to the old people of Lark Rise, where she lived:

Source 2

Flora Thompson, *Lark Rise*, 1939.

There were one or two poorer couples, just holding on to their homes, but in daily fear of the workhouse. The Poor Law authorities allowed old people past work a small weekly sum as outdoor relief; but it was not sufficient to live upon.... When, twenty years later, the Old Age Pensions began, life was transformed for such aged cottagers. They were relieved of anxiety. They were suddenly rich. Independent for life! At first when they went to the Post Office to draw it, tears of gratitude would run down the cheeks of some, and they would say as they picked up their money 'God bless that Lord George!' (for they could not believe that one so powerful and munificent (generous) could be a plain 'Mr') and God bless you, miss!...

Some historians are not impressed by the Liberal reforms:

Source 3

Arthur Marwick, *Britain in our Century*, 1984.

In my view these reforms fall within a limited, filling the gaps tradition, bearing no more than the faintest distant relationship to the idea of a comprehensive Welfare State.

Other historians have commented more favourably:

Source 4

Colin Cross, *The New British*, *The Observer*, July 1973.

David Lloyd George with his 'people's budget' of 1909 and his national health and unemployment insurance of 1911, inaugurated (started) a new political morality, now shared by all parties, that the state should intervene against gross poverty. His reforms were continued after the Second World War with the creation of what was termed 'the Welfare State'.

Source 5

Pensioners outside the post office in Wickhambrook, Suffolk, on 6 January 1908, the first day of old age pensions.

Questions

1. Read the information on pages 10–11 and make notes about the Liberal reforms of 1906–14 under the following headings. You should be able to find information about eight reforms.

Date	**Reform**	**What the reform did**	**Who was helped by it**

2. In Source 3, Arthur Marwick claims that the reforms were 'limited, filling the gaps...' Which parts of your completed table agree with this view?

3. Read Source 2.
   a How could Source 2, by itself, be used as evidence that the Pensions Act transformed the lives of the poor?
   b Look at the information on page 11 about the Pensions Act of 1909. How does this suggest that Flora Thompson's description of old age pensions was exaggerated?
   c If Flora Thompson was exaggerating, is there anything useful that Source 2 can tell us about old age pensions in 1909?

4. In Source 4, Colin Cross says that Lloyd George started 'a new political morality (way of thinking) ... that the state should intervene against gross poverty'. Judging by what you have read in Sections 1 and 2, do you think it is fair to give Lloyd George the credit for starting this way of thinking?

4 State care between the wars

The Liberal reforms of 1906–14 were halted when the First World War began. From 1914–1918 the government turned its efforts to surviving and winning the biggest war the country had ever fought. At the end of the war the government returned to the issues of care and welfare, but now with greater urgency. Over the next twenty years a mass of new laws gave the government an increasingly important part in people's lives. This section looks at how and why the state's involvement in people's welfare grew so rapidly between the two world wars.

Why and how did state care grow between the wars?

Wartime controls

During the First World War the government gained powers to control people's lives which it did not have before. The first of these powers came from the Defence of the Realm Act, or 'DORA' as people called it. Dora allowed the government to do almost anything it wanted to help it fight the war. Some of the things it did interfered in people's personal lives. For example, it changed the laws on drinking: pubs had to close in the afternoons, beer was watered down, and customers were not allowed to buy each other drinks. This was because the government believed that drunkenness was reducing the output of factory workers.

This was just one way in which the government controlled people's behaviour. Lives were also changed by the Military Service Act of 1916, which brought in compulsory service in the armed forces for men aged eighteen to 41. In 1917 the government took control of what people could eat when it introduced food rationing. It also intervened in people's working lives when it allowed women to do industrial jobs normally done by men.

Although many of these arrangements were scrapped when the war ended, people were now used to the idea that the government had a right to control certain aspects of their lives if it was in the national interest. Equally, the government became used to the idea that it could intervene in people's lives in ways it had not thought of doing before the war.

The war and pensions

The government had begun paying old age pensions in 1908. The First World War forced it into a new area of pensions. About four soldiers in every ten who saw active service in the war received wounds which disabled them (Source 1). By 1928 almost $2^1/_2$ million ex-soldiers were receiving army pensions for war wounds and disabilities.

In 1925 a new Pensions Act for old people set up a pension fund to which individuals and the government contributed. Workers paid a sum out of their weekly wage while the government made a contribution which equalled the total paid by all workers. An insured person received ten shillings (50p) a week between the ages of 65 and 70. There were also pensions for widows, children's allowances for widows, and payments for orphans.

Source 1

Disabled soldiers having artificial legs fitted at Roehampton hospital in 1918.

'Moulding a better world'

Long before the fighting ended, the government was making plans for the reconstruction of Britain at the end of the war. The Prime Minister, Lloyd George, and other ministers saw the war as an opportunity to break with the past. They said that their task was 'not so much a question of rebuilding society as it was before the war, but of moulding a better world ....' In a famous speech in 1918 Lloyd George promised 'Homes fit for heroes' for the soldiers who would shortly return from the war.

For a while it seemed that the government would succeed in 'moulding a better world'. An Education Act in 1918 provided for full-time schooling for all children aged five to fourteen: up until then eight out of ten children were finding jobs and leaving school at thirteen. Also in 1918 a Maternity and Child Welfare Act led to the building of child welfare and ante-natal clinics. In 1919 a Housing Act gave government funds to local authorities as well as private builders to build new houses. Also in 1919 a Ministry of Health was created to look after public health and health insurance.

Unemployment and state intervention

In 1920, however, Britain went into a slump. Trade dwindled and unemployment shot up. The government was forced to cut its spending on housing, health and welfare. So many workers lost their jobs that it had to alter the system of unemployment insurance it had set up in 1911. The 1911 Act covered only 2¼ out of 19 million workers, and those only for fifteen weeks in a year. After that, if they were still out of work, they had to ask the Poor Law guardians for relief.

In 1920 therefore, the government brought in a new Unemployment Insurance Act which gave benefits to all workers. In 1921 it scrapped the fifteen-week limit on payments and gave extra benefits to the wives and children of unemployed men.

The Great Depression of the 1930s put even more people out of work. By 1931, the government was spending so much on unemployment benefit (£120 million a year) that there was a financial crisis which led to the collapse of the Labour government. This was followed by cuts in benefit and the introduction of the hated means test. Testing was done by local Public Assistance Committees which took over from the Poor Law guardians in 1929.

In 1934, with unemployment still very high, the government created an Unemployment Assistance Board to take responsibility for workers who had been out of work for more than 26 weeks. This replaced the locally-run Public Assistance Committees and put the care of the long-term unemployed into the government's hands.

Planning

By the mid-1930s many people took it for granted that the government involved itself in their welfare. There was a general expectation that social problems could be dealt with by state authorities. In order to provide the services that were expected of it, the government put more and more effort into what it called 'planning'.

The idea of planning had started in the Soviet Union, whose government was taken over by Communists in 1917. One of the aims of Communism is to share a country's wealth equally among its people. The Soviet government tried to do this by planning the country's industry, agriculture, trade, and transport. A government organisation called Gosplan estimated the likely output of the country's factories and farms, and worked out ways of increasing it. From 1928 onwards, this was done through ambitious 'five-year plans' which set targets for every branch of the economy.

Governments in many countries followed the example of the Soviet Union. In Britain, many leading politicians and thinkers favoured the idea of planning because it seemed the only way to overcome the Depression and to build a fair, efficient society.

Questions

1 Look at these figures:

The percentage of the national income spent by the government on health, pensions, unemployment insurance and other social services:					
1913	5.5%	**1924**	10.3%	**1931**	15.8%

Using the information in this section, suggest reasons for the increase in these figures.

2 How did (i) the First World War, (ii) unemployment, help to bring about more government involvement in the care and welfare of British people? Which do you think was the more important in doing so?

5 A growing nation

While all these changes were taking place, the population of Britain was growing. This added to the pressure on governments to provide more care and welfare.

As Source 1 shows there are many more of us now than at the start of the century. Our numbers have risen from 38.2 million in 1901 to 55.5 million in 1991. Yet, as Source 2 shows, the average family is smaller now than in 1901. It doesn't seem to make sense. The main reason for this apparent contradiction is that people's life expectancy has steadily increased during the century (Source 3). In other words, people, are living longer than they used to. Why?

Source 1

The population of the United Kingdom, as counted in each census, 1901–1991.

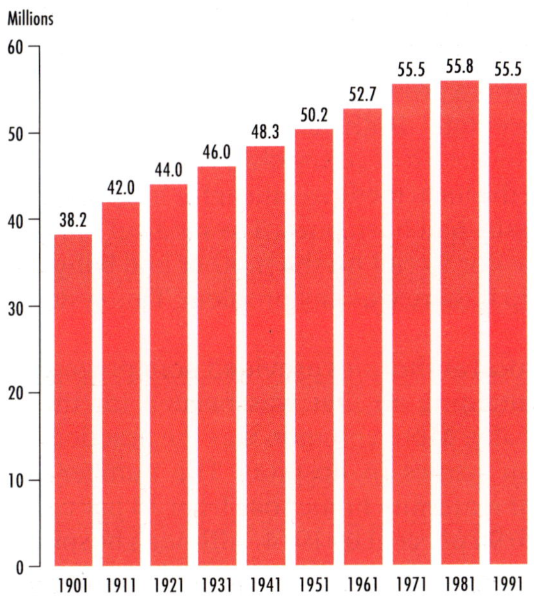

Source 2

The average size of a family, 1901–1991.

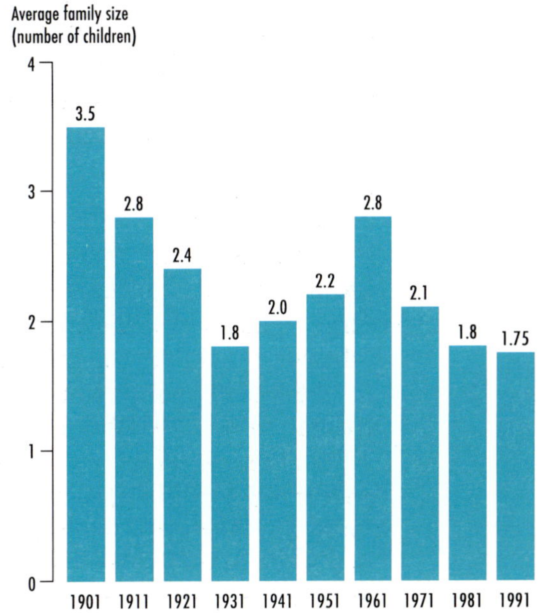

Source 3

The expectation of life at birth in the United Kingdom, 1901–1991.

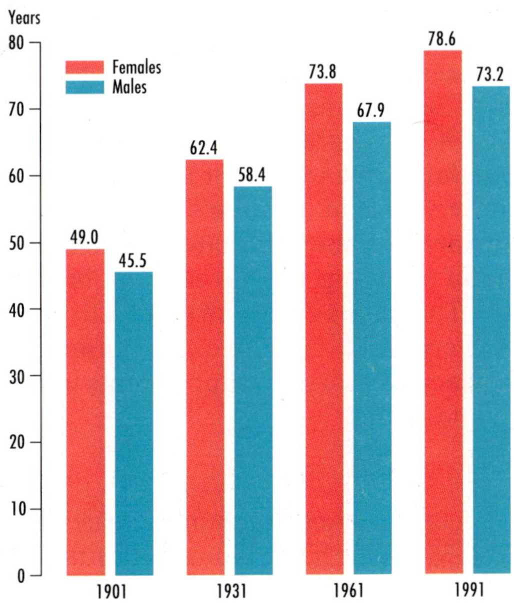

Source 4

Infant mortality in the United Kingdom, 1900–1990. (Deaths of infants under one year old per 1000 live births.)

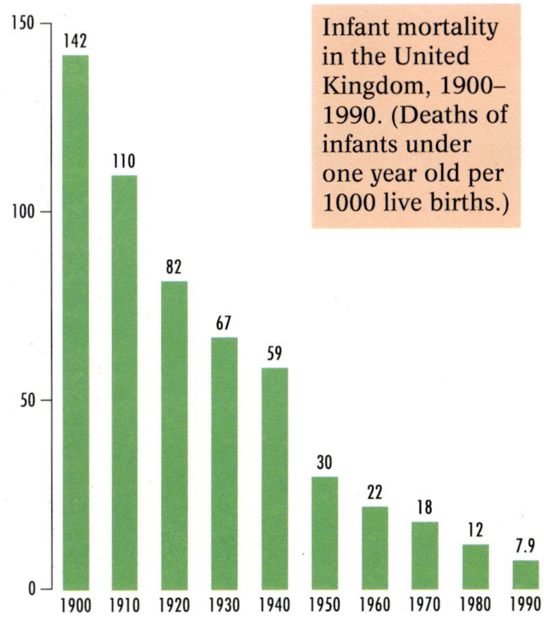

Why are people living longer?

Infant care

People are living longer firstly because the infant mortality rate has dropped. Infant mortality means the death of a baby before its first birthday. As Source 4 shows, babies at the start of the century were ten times more likely to die before their first birthday than they are today. Source 5 helps us to understand one reason why this was so. It is a description by a Glasgow midwife of the first birth she attended.

Source 5

Mary Thomson, *Stork's Nest*, an unpublished autobiography.

> My first call took me to a vermin-infested building where babies slept side by side with dogs, cats, rats, bugs, fleas and lice .... I was ushered into a room about five feet square. The patient lay on a bed built into a recess in the wall, and a line of washing – under which I had to duck – spread itself across the room. Two dogs ... occupied the space in front of the fire .... The room smelt strongly of soapsuds, bad fish, cat and dog ....

As you have read on page 7, there was a growing fear in the 1900s that the British people were becoming 'degenerate'. Both the government and local authorities took steps to improve the health of young children. In 1907 the Notification of Births Act said that the local medical officer for health must be told as soon as possible that a baby had been born. The medical officer then had to arrange for a health visitor to call on the mother and baby to check their health and arrange help if there was any problem. This system is still in use today.

Between the world wars, some local authorities provided poor pregnant women with 'maternity bags' containing all that was needed for their labour and for the delivery of the baby. More common was the practice of encouraging women to have their babies in hospital. The number of women giving birth in a hospital or maternity home rose from 15 per cent in 1927 to 54 per cent in 1946 and to 95 per cent by 1974. Although hospital delivery was often less pleasant for the mother than a home delivery, it was generally safer for the baby. Specialised help was also available if complications developed.

Child care

Children as well as babies benefited from government welfare. The act of 1906 encouraged local authorities to give poor children free school meals. Another act in 1907 set up a school medical service to provide medical inspections and, later, free treatment in schools.

Further improvements in children's health care came about during the Second World War. To make sure that children did not suffer malnutrition as a result of food rationing, the government brought in a National Milk Scheme in 1940. This gave a daily pint of milk to every pregnant or nursing mother and to every child under five (see photograph on page 22). From 1942 it also provided free vitamin supplements in the form of cod-liver oil, rose-hip syrup and orange juice.

Vaccination

People's life expectancy has been greatly increased by advances in medicine and medical care. Medicine has prolonged life firstly by preventing diseases. In the first half of the century tuberculosis (TB) was the country's biggest killer. More people died of TB than from all the other infectious diseases put together. One surgical operation in every six was to repair bones and glands rotted by TB. A major step towards fighting this awful disease was taken in 1922 when the Ministry of Health ordered that all milk be pasteurised so that TB could not be passed from dairy cattle to humans. Further progress was made after the Second World War when mobile x-ray units started touring the country to detect signs of the illness at an early stage. From the 1950s onwards, local health authorities also carried out mass vaccination campaigns, using the newly-developed BCG vaccine.

From the 1930s vaccination was also used to combat diphtheria, an often fatal infection of the throat and chest. Later, local health authorities also introduced mass vaccination against whooping cough, smallpox, scarlet fever, measles and polio. As a result of these measures, the number of people dying from infectious diseases dropped from 50 per thousand in the 1920s to less than one in a thousand in the 1970s.

New cures

From the 1930s doctors were increasingly able to cure as well as prevent killer diseases. In 1910 a German scientist developed a drug called Salvarsan to cure the sexually-transmitted disease syphilis. It was the first selective germ-killing drug. Building on the success of Salvarsan, scientists in the 1920s and 1930s developed chemical germ killers which worked in the same way – by bonding themselves to germs and killing them. Known as sulpha drugs, they could cure infectious diseases which until then usually killed people, especially the old.

Sulpha drugs, which killed one kind of germ, led to the development of a drug which could kill a wide range of germs – penicillin. Discovered by Alexander Fleming in 1928 and developed between 1938–1942 by Ernst Chain and Howard Florey, penicillin came into widespread use in 1943. Penicillin is an antibiotic drug – a substance produced by a microbe that can kill another microbe. Since the Second World War a wide range of antibiotic drugs has been developed, allowing doctors to treat most infectious diseases. Antibiotics have also made surgical operations safer by reducing the risk of post-operative infection.

Better living conditions

Compare the photograph on page 20 with the photograph on page 6. This shows us another reason why people's life expectancy increased in the twentieth century. Homes became healthier, cleaner and more comfortable as new flats and houses replaced old houses and slums. One of the most important improvements in these new homes was the provision of running water and of sewage disposal. By 1950 most homes in Britain's towns were connected to sewers and water mains, making it easier to keep them clean, to prepare food and to maintain personal hygiene.

Many people's health was also improved by a better diet. As you read on page 4, poor people in York at the start of the century mostly ate cheap 'fillers' such as bread, potatoes, stewed meat and evaporated milk. As the century went on, more and more people were able to afford fresh vegetables, fresh milk, eggs and fruit. People not only ate better, they also had to work less hard. As working hours got shorter people could spend more time on leisure activities, helping them to relax or to get exercise.

Source 6

The kitchen of a newly-built council flat in London in 1948. The flat, which was considered luxurious, had three bedrooms, a living room, bathroom and kitchen. The rent was 16s.6d. (82.5p) a week.

Questions

1 What dangers to the life of a baby can you find in Source 5?

2 Look at Source 4.

   a How many pupils are there in your year at your school?

   b If you had all been born in 1901 how many of you would have died before reaching the age of one?

   c Assume that there will be the same number of pupils in your year at your school in fifteen years time. How many of them are likely to die before reaching their fifteenth birthday?

3 Look at Source 7 and at Source 8 on pages 5–6.

   a Make a note of everything you do at home which involves the use of water.

   b If you did not have running water to do these things, how might your health be affected?

   c Why was the woman in Source 6 likely to have a healthier life than the woman in the picture on page 6?

Review: Changing care and welfare

1 Reasons for change

In 1914 a well-known economist said:

Source 1

A.C. Pigou, *Lectures on Housing*, 1914.

> The position I start from is this. It is the duty of a civilised state to lay down certain minimum conditions in every department of life, below which it does not allow any of its free citizens to fall. There must be a minimum standard of conditions in factories, a minimum standard of leisure, of dwelling accommodation, of education, of medical treatment in case of illness, and of wholesome food and clothing .... The standards must be upheld all along the line.

a What arguments can you think of to support the idea that the state (or government) has a 'duty' to provide people with minimum standards of housing, education, health, etc?
b Why did many people at the start of this century disagree with the argument that the state had this 'duty'?
c Between 1900 and 1939 the government took action to improve conditions especially for children, the elderly and the unemployed. Using pages 1–20 of this book, list the ways in which each of these three groups was helped by government action.
d There are many reasons why the government involved itself more and more in the welfare of such people. Find as many reasons as you can to explain this. Group them under these headings: political reasons; reasons to do with the economy; reasons to do with national strength; reasons to do with social justice; reasons to do with the First World War.

2 Investigation

The issues you have read about in the first part of this book are still of great concern today. Hardly a day goes by without television or newspapers carrying stories about problems connected with poverty, unemployment and welfare. Why do these problems still exist? Does it mean that little has changed since the start of the century? You can use the material in this book as the starting point for an investigation into the historical background of one of these issues.

a Begin by identifying a particular issue concerned with poverty. (For example, why are there homeless young people begging on the streets of many British cities today?) Make a collection of newspaper cuttings or video recordings about this issue.
b Try to decide why the story has got so much press coverage: why is it seen as an important issue?
c Using the material in the first part of this book, find out what similarities and differences there were between the problem of poverty today and the problem in the first part of the century?
d Display the results of your investigation e.g. mount newspaper cuttings in a wall display and write brief labels to go with them explaining the similarities and differences between the situation then and the situation today.

Focus study · Creating the Welfare State

Children of the welfare state. Five-year-olds drinking free school milk in 1947.

You have read how governments took more and more responsibility for the care and welfare of people and their families between 1900–1935. In the 1940s this led to the making of what people called the Welfare State.

In the 1940s when people talked about the Welfare State they meant a country in which the government would take a leading part in helping people to deal with any social problems that affected them. The most difficult of those problems, as we have seen, was poverty, especially when it was made worse by unemployment, old age, illness, or disability. In the Welfare State, the government would give income support, or 'social security', to help people in these situations.

Poverty was closely linked to several other social problems, especially poor health and bad housing. Helping people who lived in poverty meant dealing with these problems as well. Good, affordable medical care and decent housing were therefore also part of the Welfare State.

Underlying all these problems was the issue of work. What was the point of providing welfare benefits, free medical care and good housing if people had no jobs? In the Welfare State the government was expected to have policies which helped to provide work and avoid unemployment.

This focus study looks first at why a Welfare State was needed. The government already had welfare schemes for pensions and unemployment insurance: why were these not sufficient? We will then look at why the Welfare State was created in the 1940s and not sooner, or later; what was special about the 1940s that made it happen then? After studying the new welfare measures which the government introduced between 1945 and 1951, we ask how important these changes were, and whether they were successful.

1 The eve of the Welfare State

The picture on page 2 shows a nation wrecked by poverty. If William Booth, whose vision it was, could have seen Britain 50 years on, would he have seen any improvement? How much had changed by 1940?

How effective was welfare cover by 1940?

You have read that social insurance changed a great deal. The National Insurance scheme, started in 1911, gave health and unemployment insurance to around 12 million workers. In 1925 widows, orphans and the over-65s were included in health insurance. Further laws in the 1920s and 1930s spread health insurance cover to some 20 million people and unemployment cover to 14 million.

These insurance schemes were far from comprehensive. Health insurance entitled workers, but not their families to treatment from a panel doctor (see page 11). Workers who could afford it could pay into private insurance funds, as a Mrs Carter recalled in an interview in 1985:

Source 1

Paul Addison, *Now the War is Over*, 1985.

My husband used to pay a stamp of one and sixpence a week, a health insurance stamp for himself only, for the doctor or any medication he would need and he also paid a scheme at work, threepence a week, which was called a hospital scheme and that covered the whole family for any hospitalisation that was needed, but not maternity. I paid threepence a week into a medical aid for my son, but I was in good health so I didn't bother about myself.

Many people could not keep up the payments on private insurance schemes. People without insurance cover therefore avoided visits to the doctor unless it was absolutely necessary. The wife of a Yorkshire miner, talking in the 1980s, remembered:

Source 2

Stuart Archer and Nigel Shepley, *Witnessing History*, 1988

I had my daughter before the 1939 war. At the maternity home we had to pay £2 deposit and another ten shillings when she came. I got up at six in the morning and said to my husband, 'Come on, we're ready'. I had to walk down to the maternity home with a hole in my shoe ....

I never went to the doctor's. There was a post-natal clinic, but I didn't go .... We got no help at all with anything.

Women who neglected their health because they could not afford treatment often suffered later in life. A Scottish doctor, looking back to the 1940s, remembered that:

Source 3

Doctor Alastair Clarke, *The Independent*, 4 July 1988.

People always managed to find the money to bring in their children. But the mothers would go without. When the National Health Service (and free medical treatment) came in, all that emerged. Within six months I had 30 or 40 women come in who had been suffering gynaecological problems*, many of them for years ....

gynaecological problems
Diseases and disorders of the female reproductive system.

It wasn't only doctors who were too expensive for many people to visit. Dentists' fees were so high that people usually only went to get aching teeth pulled out, not to have check-ups. Opticians' fees were so high that people who needed glasses had to buy them in shops like Woolworths. In Source 4, a Mr Law remembers his father buying spectacles from Woolworths in Manchester Piccadilly.

Source 4

Paul Addison, *Now the War is Over*, 1985.

Stacked on the counter were spectacles with a large card with a large A going down to a small Z ... and I can see my father now, trying on different pairs of glasses, looking at the card, putting down, picking another pair up, until he got the selected pair he required, then he would look at me, he would ask me how he looked. I'd say, 'You look smashing, Dad,' and then we'd just go out of the store.

Source 5

A page from one of a series of feature articles about unemployment in *Picture Post* magazine in 1939. It followed unemployed Alfred Smith in his search for work.

PICTURE POST

Vol. 2. No. 3. January 21, 1939

I *Before the Labour Exchange : One of 1,830,000 Workless*

There are over 1,830,000 Unemployed in Great Britain. From a group outside Peckham Labour Exchange we picked out one, Alfred Smith (X) and followed him with the camera. On the following pages is the story of his daily routine.

UNEMPLOYED!

Britain is a rich country. But at the beginning of this year, it had 1,831,372 registered unemployed, and many more not registered. This was 3,269 more than in November, 1938, 165,965 more than a year ago. In two years, the figures have risen by 207,770. Is this volume of unemployment necessary?

ALFRED SMITH lives at 52, Leo Street, Peckham. He is a little man, thin, but wiry, with the pale face and bright eyes of a real Londoner. He wears a cloth cap and white muffler, old brown jacket and corduroy trousers. He talks animatedly, likes a joke, walks with his hands in his pockets, shoulders bent, head slightly forward. And he looks down as he walks—the typical walk of an unemployed man.

His face is lined, and his cheeks are sunken, because he has no teeth. He is only 35 years old.

He has a wife and four children.

He has not had a regular job for three years.

When Alfred Smith married 12 years ago, he was a skilled workman, a spray enamel maker, earning good wages. Things went well with him for nine years. But then the chemicals used in this work made his teeth rot, so that they had to be

PICTURE POST 11

Like health insurance, unemployment insurance had its limitations. After receiving sixteen weeks of benefit, an unemployed worker had to go on the 'dole', like Alfred Smith in Source 5. This was hard enough, but unemployed people who had no insurance could only get help from the local Public Assistance Committees (PAC) which took over from the Poor Law Guardians in 1929. In an interview in 1988 Violet Harris remembered the help her family got from the PAC in Lambeth in London:

Source 6

Mary Chamberlain, *Growing up in Lambeth*, 1989.

They used to give you what they called parish relief, served it out on the premises, along the Kennington Lane, right opposite the police station there. They used to give you some meat, black as your hat. True. Potatoes, with whiskers all growing out of them. Black sugar. Black, almost, bread. Yards of treacle and blooming old car grease supposed to be margarine, you know. But you never got a penny off them.

When the Depression began, the only people who got to know about the misery of unemployment were the unemployed and their families and neighbours. By the late 1930s, most people knew something about it. Newspapers and magazines increasingly gave space to the social problems of the Depression. Magazines like *Picture Post* used what they called 'photojournalism' to give these stories maximum impact. The photograph opposite, which appeared in *Picture Post* in 1939, was typical of the new photojournalism, and helped to create an unforgettable image of the Depression for the magazine's readers.

Questions

1 Judging by Sources 1–6 in this section what gaps and shortcomings were there in welfare provision in the 1930s?

2 Why did more people know about poverty and other social problems in 1939 than in 1900?

2 War and welfare

By 1939 public opinion was firmly in favour of a major expansion of social services. Opinion did not change when Britain went to war with Germany in September 1939. In fact the opposite happened. Over the next five and a half years of war, demands for government action on social problems grew louder and louder. The government could not ignore these demands, and drew up plans for new health and insurance schemes. Between 1944 and 1948 these plans were put into practice with the passing of major new National Insurance, National Health, and National Assistance Acts. These acts together created 'the Welfare State'.

It might seem surprising that the Welfare State was planned and partly created during the Second World War. You might expect the government to have dropped welfare plans so that it could concentrate on the war effort. Why did the war speed up instead of slow down the expansion of the social services?

How did the war help to accelerate reform?

The changing mood of the nation

The Second World War changed the way in which British people thought about their society and about the future of the country. Public opinion surveys showed that most people hoped for a better world after the war than the depressed world of the 1930s. This new mood can be explained by several wartime developments.

1 The war brought people together. For five and a half years millions of men and women shared experiences such as evacuation or service in the Home Guard or rescue services. They shared hardships such as food rationing and they sheltered together during air raids. This not only broke down the barriers between people of different social classes. It also gave people a sense of fighting together in a common cause.

2 The war forced the government to involve itself more closely in social services. For example, to make sure that hospitals could cope with war casualties, the government brought most hospitals under its control through the Emergency Hospital Scheme. It also introduced food supplements to protect children from malnutrition as a result of food rationing. From 1940 onwards it provided children with free school milk and later with free orange juice, cod-liver oil and vitamin tablets.

3 The war opened many people's eyes to the poverty of Britain's cities. Many of the 1.5 million women and children evacuated in 1939 were from poor working class families. Source 1 describes the condition of some of the children.

Source 1

The National Federation of Women's Institutes, *Town Children Through Country Eyes*, 1941.

> In practically every batch of children there were some who suffered from head-lice, skin diseases and bed-wetting .... Some children (from Manchester) had never slept in beds before .... One boy (from Salford) had never had a bath before .... The state of the children (from Liverpool) was such that the school had to be fumigated after reception .... Few (Manchester) children would eat food that demanded the use of teeth – could only eat with a teaspoon .... One little girl of five (from Liverpool) remarked that she would like to have beer and cheese for supper .... Some (Gosport) children had never used a knife and fork ....

People's hopes for a better world were reflected in a huge number of plans, drawn up during the war, for postwar reconstruction. Political parties, churches, universities and local councils drew up detailed plans for postwar Britain. One such plan was put forward by the popular magazine, *Picture Post*, in January 1941. It demanded a job for everybody, minimum wages, child allowances, social insurance, a health service and new housing. Source 2, taken from its housing plan, gives us an idea of how some people saw the future in 1941.

The Beveridge Plan

The most famous wartime plan was an instant bestseller when it came out in December 1942. One hundred thousand copies of Sir William Beveridge's *Social Insurance and Allied Services* were bought in December alone. Beveridge was a senior civil servant who had been involved in social policy

Source 2

A drawing in *Picture Post's* new year issue in 1941, *A Plan for Britain*, shows its proposals for the rebuilding of Britain's towns and cities.

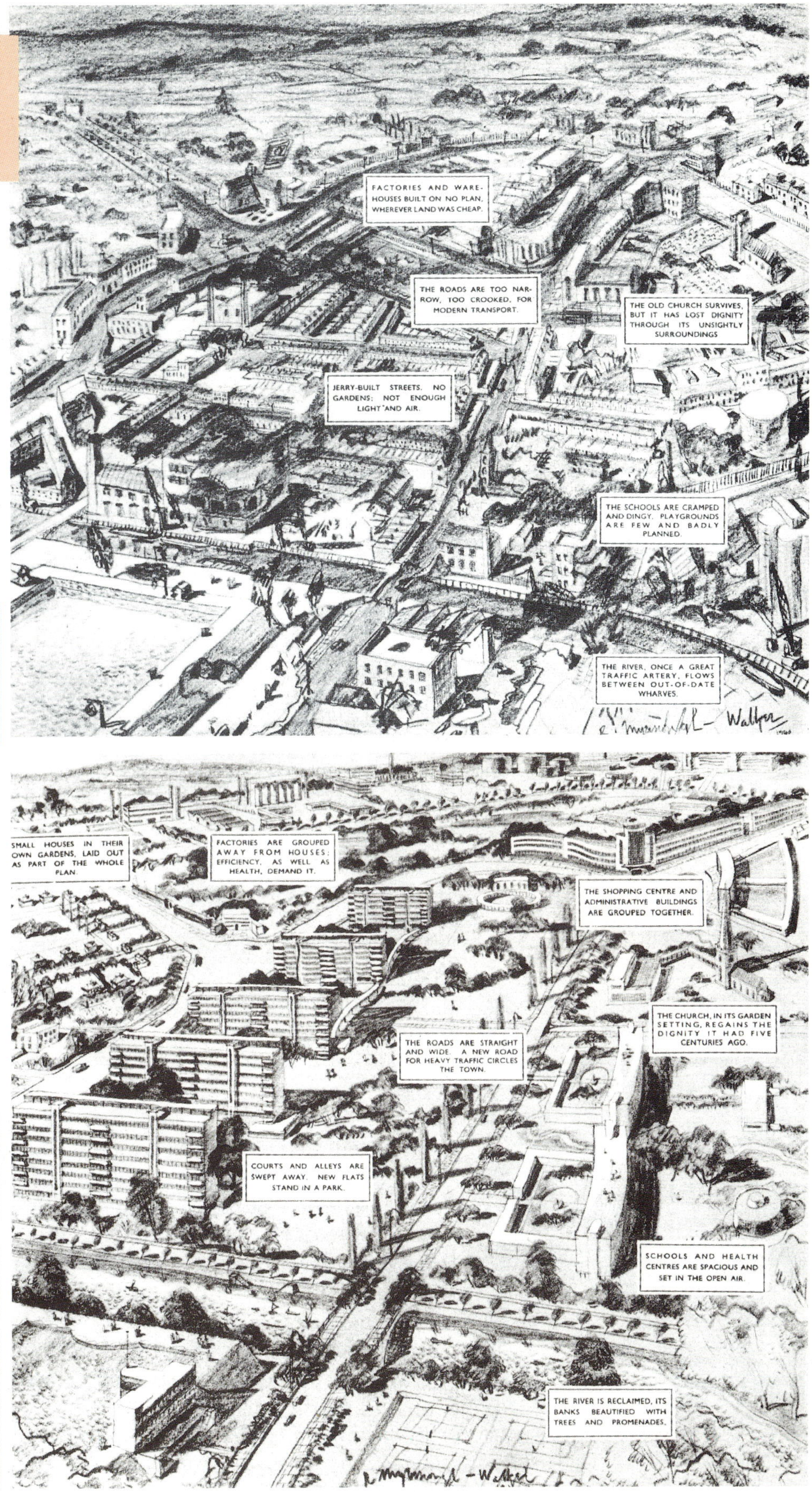

Source 3

Sir William Beveridge making a speech about his Social Insurance proposals at a Liberal Party meeting in 1943.

for many years. He had, for example, helped to set up the National Insurance scheme of 1912. In 1941 he was made chairman of a government Committee on Social Insurance to look into the various insurance schemes that existed and to suggest how to improve them. In his report, however, Beveridge made suggestions about more than just insurance. In the famous introduction to the Report, he explained that social problems were all linked:

Source 4

Report by Sir William Beveridge, *Social Insurance and Allied Services*, 1942.

A revolutionary moment in the world's history is a time for revolutions, not for patching.

... Social insurance should be treated as one part only of a comprehensive policy of social progress. Social insurance fully developed may provide income security; it is an attack on Want. But Want is only one of five giants on the road of reconstruction and in some ways the easiest to attack. The others are Disease, Ignorance, Squalor and Idleness.

In his report, Beveridge went on to say that there should be a single insurance system. People should make weekly contributions to a government-run insurance scheme that would protect them 'from the cradle to the grave'. The scheme would provide:

- benefits for the unemployed, sick and disabled
- pensions and benefits for old people, widows and orphans
- funeral grants
- maternity benefits.

Anybody not covered by the scheme would be maintained by a system of National Assistance. Underpinning all this, Beveridge expected that the government would provide family allowances, create a national health service and maintain full employment.

However, the government did not act immediately to put the Beveridge Plan into operation. The Prime Minister, Winston Churchill, worried not only about the cost, but also that the plan would 'raise false hopes'. Nevertheless, the plan was so popular that the government was forced to set up a Reconstruction Committee to plan Britain's post-war future. From 1943-45 this committee brought out a series of White Papers, proposing major changes in education, health, employment policy, social insurance and housing.

Source 5

A Labour Party election poster of 1945 uses the famous wartime V for victory symbol to encourage voters to 'win the peace'.

The 1945 election

Throughout the war the government of Britain was a coalition, led from May 1940 onwards by Winston Churchill. The idea was that the Conservative, Labour and Liberal parties would put aside their differences for as long as the war lasted to work together for the war effort.

In May 1945 Germany surrendered, bringing the war in Europe to an end. Churchill and the Labour leader, Clement Attlee, agreed to hold a general election without delay. The date was fixed for 5 July 1945.

In the election campaign, the Conservatives promised that they would introduce all the measures outlined in the White Papers of 1945. However, Churchill warned voters that the country was in a difficult economic position and that introducing these measures quickly would be hard. In contrast, the Labour Party promised to enact the White Paper proposals without delay. It also promised other measures designed to modernise Britain: the nationalisation of coal, gas, electricity, the railways, iron and steel.

The election result was a landslide victory for the Labour Party. Labour won 393 seats against the Conservatives 213. With a majority of 183 over all other parties put together, it was able to start putting its promises into effect without delay.

Questions

1 Read Source 1. How might the experience of looking after children like these have changed the way people thought about the subject of poverty?

2 Look at Source 2. What does this drawing tell you about the kind of Britain some people hoped for at the end of the war?

3 **a** In Source 4, Beveridge identified five 'giants': what were they?
b These were rather old fashioned words to describe modern problems: suggest five modern words which mean the same.
c Why should Beveridge have thought that 1942 was 'a revolutionary moment in the world's history'?

4 Beveridge was not a good speech-maker (Source 3), yet he was asked to give many speeches in 1942–43. Suggest why he was in such demand.

5 Using the sources and information in this section, give as many reasons as you can to explain why the war led to demands for more state provision of welfare.

3 The birth of the Welfare State

Source 1

A mother collects the Family Allowance from a post office in 1946.

The new Labour government's first action was to put into effect an act of the wartime coalition government, the Family Allowances Act. All mothers were issued with books of coupons which they could cash at the local post office (Source 1). The coupons were worth five shillings (25p) a week for each child after the first.

The rest of Beveridge's proposals were made into law by four Acts of Parliament:

- The National Insurance Act, 1946
- The National Health Service Act, 1946
- The Industrial Injuries Act, 1946
- The National Assistance Act, 1946

Much complex planning was needed before these Acts could be put into operation. The date fixed for the start of a new National Insurance scheme, a National Health Service and a National Assistance Board was 5 July 1948. The government called it 'The Appointed Day'. Ever since it has been taken as the day when the Welfare State was born – a key date and a key event in Britain's history.

'The Appointed Day': a turning point?

People at the time believed that something was about to change on 'the Appointed Day':

Source 2

The Daily Mail, 3 July 1948.

> On Monday morning you will wake up in a New Britain, in a State which 'takes over' its citizens six months before they are born, providing care and free services for their birth, for their early years, their schooling, sickness, workless days, widowhood, and retirement. Finally, it helps defray the cost of their departure. All this, with free doctoring, dentistry and medicine – free bath chairs, too, if needed – for 4s 11d out of your weekly pay packet. You begin paying next Friday.

National Insurance

The payments of 4s 11d (25p) were contributions to a National Insurance scheme. After the 'Appointed Day', all workers (except married women) had to pay for a weekly insurance stamp costing 4s 11d which was stuck onto his or her National Insurance card. The government and the employer also paid contributions towards the stamp. Having a paid-up card entitled the holder to sickness and unemployment benefits, retirement and widows' pensions, maternity benefit and a funeral allowance. The benefits were all flat-rate, meaning that everyone got the same amounts. For pensioners this was 42 shillings a week for a married couple, compared with 20 shillings before. Unemployment pay for a man was 26 shillings a week, with a further sixteen shillings a week for a wife and 7s 6d for each child. James Griffiths, the Minister of National Insurance, said that this was 'the best and cheapest insurance policy offered to any people anywhere'.

With 25 million workers in Britain in 1948, this scheme was on a gigantic scale. The Ministry of National Insurance which ran it had 40,000 staff in newly-built offices in Newcastle. The records of insured workers were kept on 25 million sheets stored in 100 rooms. (Computers had not yet been invented to store such information.) Among those records were the details of 650,000 men and women named Smith, of whom 8,000 were all called John Smith. Throughout the country 992 local offices handled claims for benefit and passed them on to the headquarters in Newcastle.

National Assistance

People not in paid work – for example, the disabled, the homeless, or unmarried mothers – could not receive National Insurance benefits, nor could workers with insufficient stamps. These people could apply for help to a new National Assistance Board. Although there was a means test for help, it was a test on the claimant only, not the whole family. As one minister in the government said, 'At last we have buried the old Poor Law'.

The National Health Service

The National Health Service which came into existence on 5 July 1948 made four major changes to the existing system of health care.

- **All medical treatment was to be free** for everybody, whether or not they had National Insurance stamps.

- **Doctors were to be paid by the state**: hospital doctors received a salary, while General Practitioners received a fee for every patient on their lists, whether or not they treated them.
- **Three thousand hospitals were nationalised** and put under the control of fourteen regional hospital groups.
- **Local authorities had to provide free medical services**; for example, home nurses, midwives, infant care, immunisation, and ambulance services.

The impact of the Welfare State

These new welfare measures took rapid effect. Source 3 describes how the introduction of the National Health Service affected a family in Leeds.

Source 3

Mrs Clare Bond, from Leeds, interviewed in 1985 in Paul Addison, *Now the War is Over*, 1985.

gas and air Nitrous oxide and oxygen – a recently introduced form of pain relief used in childbirth.

... oh, it was fantastic. My mother and dad had been having problems with their teeth for ages, and I think they were first at the dentist, as soon as he opened .... Instead of having just a few teeth out, they had the complete set out, and free dentures. You know? Thought it was wonderful .... My sister had had school-supply steel-rimmed spectacles for ages .... As soon as the NHS started she was there, (at the) optician. Marvellous NHS spectacles, you know, some style about them .... And then I had another sister, she'd had one baby and it was rather bad, she had to pay 12s 6d for a midwife, no gas and air*, anything like this, and just after the NHS started she had her second baby, at home .... Then she thought it was absolutely wonderful, because besides having a free midwife, she had a nurse come in every day ... bathed the baby, showed her how to look after it.

At a press conference in October 1949 the Minister for Health, Aneurin Bevan, gave figures to show what use had been made of the National Health Service since the 'Appointed Day'.

- 187 million prescriptions had been dispensed at 2s9d (14p) each.
- 5.25 million pairs of glasses had been supplied. Three million more were on order.
- 8.5 million dental patients had been accepted for treatment.

Seebohm Rowntree, whose research into poverty in York in 1901 you read about on page 4, conducted further surveys of poverty in York over the following half century, the last in 1951. The results were startling:

Source 4

Seebohm Rowntree, *Poverty. A Study of Town Life*, 1901, and Seebohm Rowntree and G.R. Lavers, 1951.

Poverty in York 1901–1951

	Percentage of working-class families living in poverty	**Percentage of the whole population of York living in poverty**
1901	43.4%	27.8
1936	31.1%	18.0
1951	2.8%	1.5

Source 5

An optician fits a schoolgirl with free National Health Service spectacles in February 1951.

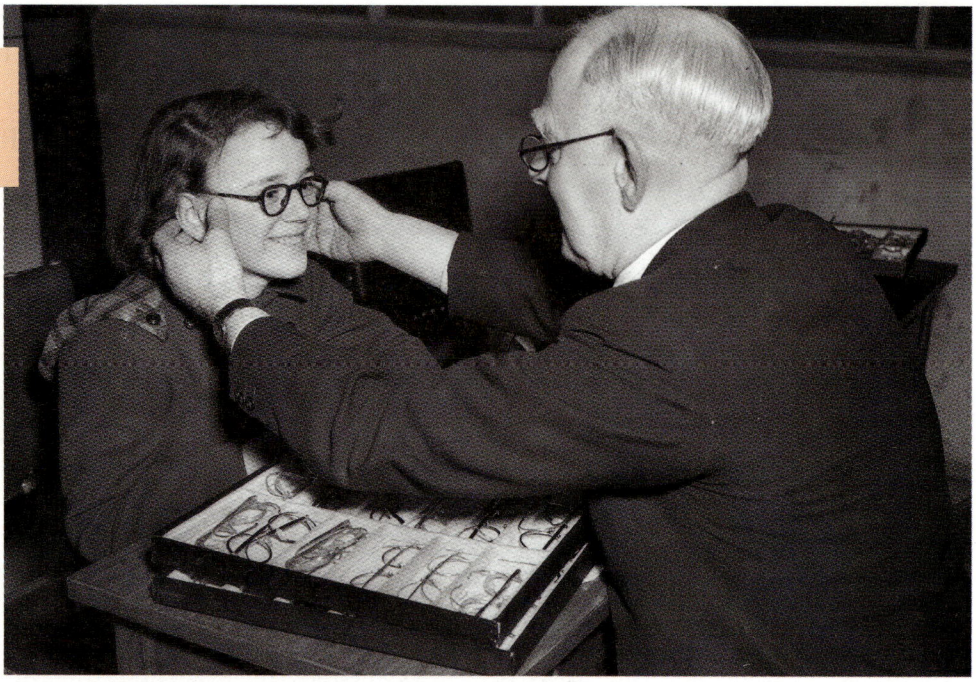

Questions

1. In Source 2 the *Daily Mail* told its readers that they would wake up in 'a New Britain' on 5 July 1948. Using the information in this section, say what changed in Britain on 5 July 1948.
2. How can the information in this section be used to support the idea that 'a New Britain' was born on 5 July 1948?

4 Bevan and the doctors

After reading how patients flocked to use the National Health Service in 1948, you might think that doctors welcomed the birth of the Welfare State. Not so. There were doctors who angrily opposed the NHS from the moment the Beveridge Plan first appeared in 1942. From 1942–1948 they fought a fierce battle to stop the creation of the health service.

The main target of the doctors' attacks was the Labour Minister for Health from 1945–1951, Aneurin Bevan. For three years Bevan and the doctors argued angrily about the future of the country's health. What was at stake? Why could they not agree on an issue that seemed to be in everybody's interests? Why were their arguments so heated?

The National Health Service: for and against

At first the doctors had been in favour of a National Health Service. They set up a Medical Planning Commission during the war and in 1942 issued a report calling for a health service covering the whole country. This was to include the building of health centres, the payment of doctors by the state, and the reorganisation of hospitals.

However, their attitude changed after the Beveridge Report appeared in 1942. When they learned in 1943 that the government was planning to create a health service along the lines suggested by Beveridge, they protested:

Source 1

British Medical Journal, 1943.

If this happens, then doctors will no longer be an independent, learned and liberal profession, but will instead form a service of technicians controlled by bureaucrats and by local men and women entirely ignorant of medical matters.

Up to 1945 the ideas for creating a national health service came from a Conservative Minister of Health. The Labour victory in the 1945 general election put the Ministry of Health under Labour control. The new Minister of Health was Aneurin Bevan, MP for Ebbw Vale in Wales.

Source 2

Aneurin Bevan, Minister of Health from 1945–48, visiting the tuberculosis centre at Papworth Hospital in May 1948.

Aneurin Bevan

Aneurin Bevan – or Nye as he was known – was born in 1897 in the mining town of Tredegar in South Wales. He was the sixth of ten children, but only eight of his brothers and sisters survived infancy and only six reached adulthood. He left school at the age of thirteen to work in the local coal mine, and worked at the coal face for the next nine years.

The experience of working in the pit – of danger, long hours and low pay – made him despise the mine owners. He joined the miners' trade union and, at nineteen, became leader of the local branch. He quickly gained a reputation as a militant and in 1926 he led the Welsh miners in the General Strike. During the 1920s he was also out of work for two years.

Bevan's dislike of the mine owners grew when his father died of pneumoconiosis in 1925. This lung disease, which cements up the air passages in the lungs, was caused by a lifetime of breathing coal dust beneath the ground. Bevan later wrote in his autobiography:

Source 3

Aneurin Bevan, *In Place of Fear*, 1952.

No compensation was paid him by the mine owners; in those days it was not scheduled as an industrial disease under the Workmen's Compensation Acts.

In 1929 Bevan became a Member of Parliament, first as a member of the Independent Labour Party, then after 1931 as a member of the more moderate Labour Party. He became Minister of Health following the Labour election victory of 1945. He did not, however, forget his experiences as a young man. In a famous speech in 1948, he told Labour supporters about the time when he was unemployed in the 1920s He went on:

Source 4

Speech in Manchester, reported in *The Times*, 5 July 1948.

That is why no amount of cajolery (sweet-talking) ... can eradicate from my heart a deep burning hatred for the Tory Party that inflicted these experiences on me. So far as I am concerned they are lower than vermin. They condemned millions of first-class people to semi-starvation.

The NHS Bill

In 1945 Bevan drew up a National Health Service bill. Bevan's bill went further than the plans of his Conservative predecessor. Four new proposals alarmed the doctors. Bevan planned to put all hospitals under the control of thirteen regional boards directed by the Ministry of Health. He wanted doctors to be paid a salary rather than fees for each of their patients. He wanted to stop doctors setting up new practices in areas where there were already enough doctors, and to encourage them into areas with too few doctors. He also wanted to abolish the right of doctors to buy and sell practices (and thus patients.) The cartoon in Source 5 reflects the worries of the doctors.

Source 5

A cartoon by 'Vicky' shows Aneurin Bevan, the new Minister of Health, walking along Harley Street, the famous London street where wealthy medical specialists and consultants have their practices.

HERE HE COMES, BOYS!

These proposals so angered the doctors that Bevan decided he had to tone them down. He began by making concessions to the most powerful doctors, the consultants who belonged to the Royal Colleges of Surgeons, Physicians and Obstetricians. He said they would be able to work part-time in the NHS, that they could charge fees to their private patients, and that they could have private hospital beds for their private patients in NHS hospitals. Privately, Bevan said he was 'stuffing their mouths with gold'.

This left the 51,000 general practitioners of the British Medical Association to deal with. Some members of the BMA were deeply suspicious of Bevan. Source 6 tell what one of them said about the NHS Bill.

Source 6

Michael Foot, *Aneurin Bevan*. Volume 2 1945–60 (1973).

The Bill can be written in two lines: "I hereby take powers to do what I like about the medical service of the country – signed Nye Bevan, fuehrer.*

Fuehrer The official title of Adolf Hitler, Nazi dictator of Germany from 1933 to 1945.

The BMA could not stop Parliament from making the NHS Bill into law in 1946, but it could try to stop its members from joining the NHS. In 1947 it organised a vote of its members in which 40,814 doctors voted against the Act and only 4,735 in favour. The NHS could not possibly work with only 4,735 doctors, so Bevan was forced to make a concession. He announced that he would add to the NHS Act a promise that doctors would never be paid wholly by salaries. At the same time he started a publicity campaign to persuade people to register with a NHS doctor. A doctor who refused to accept registrations risked losing patients to a doctor who would.

In these ways, Bevan persuaded many doctors to drop their opposition to the NHS. By the 'appointed day' for the start of the NHS, nine out of every ten GPs had joined it.

Questions

1. How does Bevan's early life help us to understand why he wanted a National Health Service under state control?
2. What do Sources 1 and 6 tell us about why the British Medical Association opposed the creation of the National Health Service?

5 Problems and achievements of the Welfare State

The arguments about the National Health Service did not stop after it was created in 1948. The NHS was immediately faced with many difficult problems. The social security schemes of National Insurance and National Assistance also ran into difficulties. This section looks at why the newly-formed Welfare State faced so many problems, and asks whether this meant that it was a failure.

Did the Welfare State succeed?

Problems of the NHS

The planners who created the NHS assumed that there was a backlog of untreated illnesses which could be cleared up very quickly – people with bad teeth or poor eyesight, for example. Once these had been treated, the planners thought, the number of patients would quickly fall.

They were wrong. Patients came in growing numbers throughout the 1950s to receive free medical treatment. One reason for this was that the

Source 1

Nine months after the creation of the NHS, out-patients at the London Hospital in Whitechapel queue to see doctors, to make appointments and to collect prescriptions.

people most likely to need medical treatment – children and old people – were increasing in numbers faster than the rest of the population. In the case of pensioners, this was because new drugs and advances in surgery helped to cure old people of illnesses such as pneumonia that previously would have killed them. Source 1 shows one of the National Health Service's biggest problems – too many patients.

The huge demand for treatment led to an explosion in the costs of the NHS. Medicines especially cost more than expected. Instead of an expected 50 million, doctors wrote 227 million prescriptions for drugs in 1951. NHS spending rose so fast that the government decided in 1951 to charge patients for part of the cost of glasses and false teeth. In 1952 it also introduced charges for prescriptions and dental treatment.

The introduction of health charges did not reduce the demand for medical care. During the 1950s and 1960s there were many advances in what doctors could do for their patients. New drugs such as penicillin allowed them to control infections. New anaesthetics allowed surgeons to perform longer and more complex operations. Naturally, the more that doctors were able to do, the more their patients came to them for treatment.

In the 1950s the government tried to keep tight control of all its spending and it limited pay increases for many state-paid workers. This had a serious effect on the NHS. While long waiting lists for hospital treatment built up, 57,000 hospital beds were empty because there was a shortage of nurses, caused mainly by low pay. Government controls on its spending also meant that no new hospitals were built during the 1950s.

Despite its problems, few people wanted to turn the clock back. A public opinion survey of 1956 found that 90 per cent of the population thought the NHS was a good service, with 7 per cent undecided and only 3 per cent against it. On the tenth anniversary of the NHS, *The Times* newspaper said that:

Source 2

The Times, 7 July 1958.

... it has been criticised in detail, but the concept as such has not been seriously challenged. Mistakes have been made, but an impartial review of the past ten years indicates that the nation has good reason to be proud of the Health Service.

Problems of social security

The social security schemes of 1948 (National Insurance and National Assistance) also ran into difficulties. The first problem was that the cash benefits provided by National Insurance were too small for many people to live on, especially the old. When they were introduced in 1948 they were already smaller than the benefits Beveridge had recommended in his Report. In the 1950s inflation reduced their value further. By 1953 one in four widows and old people were having to ask for National Assistance to supplement their pensions.

Benefits were not only small but also flat-rate: everyone got the same regardless of their needs. While poor people were getting benefits too small to live on, people who did not really need them also had a right to the same benefits. The Conservative governments of the 1950s questioned whether this was a good use of government money. Source 3, written by a leading economist, summed up this view:

Source 3

W. Hagenbuch, *The Rationale of the Social Services*, 1953.

Social services were originally intended to provide services for the poorest members of the community; now they have become the providers of universal services, free for everyone, on an ever-increasing scale.

In 1959 the government therefore brought in graduated insurance payments. Instead of paying flat-rate contributions, workers now paid according to their earnings. The more they earned, the bigger their contributions; and the bigger the contribution, the bigger the pension. In this way the government was able to increase pensions without having to spend more.

The next major change to social security came in 1966 when a Labour government scrapped the National Assistance Board and replaced it with a Supplementary Benefits scheme. This was meant to give benefits to those who most needed them. Supplementary Benefits increased claimants' incomes on a scale that took into account such things as the number and age of their children, and gave them a rent allowance. By 1980 more than 5 million people receiving National Insurance were also drawing Supplementary Benefits.

The cost of welfare

The cost of welfare was enormous. Source 4 shows how spending on social services has increased during the twentieth century. You can easily see that spending has risen faster and faster since the introduction of the Welfare State.

The most expensive of those services was social security. The rocketing costs of social security led some people, especially those in the Conservative Party, to question its very existence. They also argued that the Welfare State was taking away from many people a sense of responsibility for looking after themselves and their families. The example they gave most often to illustrate this problem was the 'social security scrounger'. From the 1950s onwards, stories went round of people claiming benefits they were not entitled to. Such stories became common after the introduction of Supplementary Benefits in 1966 when, despite complex rules to ensure against it, some people found they could earn nearly as much in benefits as they could if they were working.

In 1980 the Conservative government declared that public spending was the main cause of Britain's economic difficulties. Social services was the biggest item of spending, and the government therefore set about reducing it. In 1980, for example, it stopped increasing old age pensions at the same rate of inflation, saving 4 billion pounds a year.

Despite such cuts, in 1990 the Welfare State was still receiving the same share of Britain's income as it was in 1980. As Source 4 shows, half the government's spending was on social services. This was because a massive rise in unemployment led to several million more people claiming unemployment benefits. At the same time, it seemed to many people that poverty was becoming more serious and more widespread than at any time since the start of the Welfare State. Scenes like that in Source 5 seem to show that poverty in Britain in the 1990s is still a major social problem.

Source 4

The percentage of Britain's income used to pay for health, social security, education, housing and other social services.

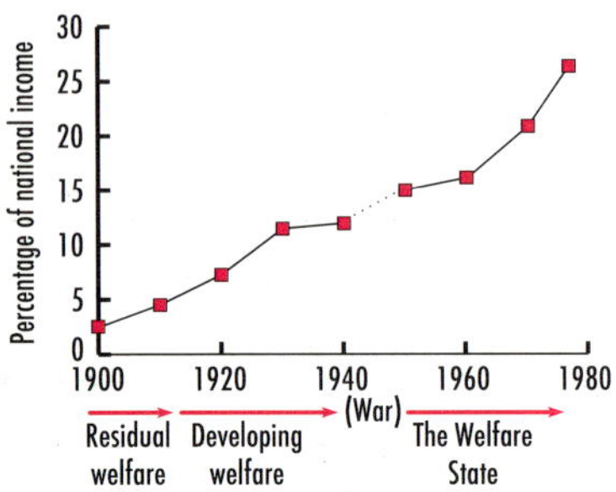

Source 5

This photograph appeared in *The Guardian*, a left-of-centre newspaper, in June 1993. It showed 22-year-old James Flood, unemployed since leaving school, begging in a street in Manchester.

Questions

1 *The Times* (Source 2) said that 'mistakes have been made' in the National Health Service.

a Use the information in this section to give examples of 'mistakes' in the first ten years of the NHS.

b An opinion poll in 1956 found that 90 per cent of the British people supported the NHS. In view of the 'mistakes' you have listed, how might this be explained?

2 Source 5 shows a man begging in the street. Does this prove that the Welfare State has not succeeded in wiping out poverty in Britain?

Review: The Welfare State

Historians do not always agree about the history of the Welfare State. They differ chiefly on two questions. First, was the creation of the Welfare State a revolution, or was it created by a gradual process? In other words, was it the product of revolution or evolution? Second, who, if anyone, deserves the credit for creating it?

Revolution or evolution?

Forty years after the start of the Welfare State, a civil servant looked back to when he started work in the newly-created Ministry of Health:

Source 1

Patrick Benner, *The Early Years of the National Health Service – an Insider's View*, 1989.

To me ... it seemed at the time that the process must have been revolutionary rather than evolutionary, and that there was a great cataclysm in 1946–48 as a result of which an entirely new service had been brought to birth.

In 1990 a historian wrote:

Source 2

Michael Rawcliffe. *The Welfare State*, 1990.

The Welfare State was essentially the culmination of half a century of piecemeal social reform now carried to its logical conclusion.

1. Look at pages 30–31. What was there about the National Health Service in 1948 that could be described as 'entirely new'?
2. Look at pages 11, 18 and 19. What health services already existed by 1948?
3. Look at pages 10–11, 14–16 and 24. Give examples of 'social reforms' that had been made over the half century before 1948.
4. How much progress do you consider these reforms made in the provision of welfare? Explain your answer.
5. Using the information in this book, say whether you agree with Source 1 (that the Welfare State was a revolution) or with Source 2 (that it was a result of evolution.) Explain your answer.

Source 3

This cartoon appeared on 5 July 1948 in *The Daily Herald*, a left-wing newspaper which supported the Labour Party.

BRITAIN'S QUADS: *First family album picture*

Who created the Welfare State?

In this book you have read about the involvement of many people in the subject of welfare. Some were politicians. Some were writers who drew attention to the subject of poverty and some were civil servants. There were also many less famous people; doctors, researchers and journalists, for example. Which, if any, played the biggest part in creating the Welfare State?

Source 3 gives one answer. The cartoonist George Whitelaw showed Aneurin Bevan, the Minister of Health, and James Griffiths, the Minister of National Insurance, as the proud fathers of the Welfare State.

Another newspaper, *The Times*, which claimed not to support any one party, wrote on the tenth anniversary of the National Health Service:

Source 4

The Times Supplement on the National Health Service, 7 July 1958.

Conceived by a Liberal, nurtured by a Coalition government under a Conservative Prime Minister, and brought to health by a Labour government, the National Health Service can justly claim to be a national institution.

Credit for creating the Welfare State could also be given to individuals much earlier in the century (Source 5).

Source 5

Colin Cross, *Making a start on the Welfare State*, in *The Observer Magazine*, July 1973.

Probably the greatest contribution ever made to British society by an individual politician has been that of David Lloyd George.

Professor Ben Pimlott wrote that:

Source 6

Ben Pimlott, review in *The Guardian*, 31 October 1992.

It is an amusing parlour game to guess what might have happened but for (the Second World War); presumably the Tories would have won an election in 1939 or 1940 and there would have been no Welfare State .... The wartime shake-up in Whitehall (was) 'Hitler's revolution'. There is certainly a sense in which it was Hitler's Beveridge Report; and today ... we still benefit from the Führer's council houses and secondary schools, social services and free hospital care.

Questions

1. Look at Source 3. What did Griffiths and Bevan do to change welfare provision in 1948?
2. **a** Read Source 4. Using pages 28, 34 and 39, identify (i) the 'Liberal', (ii) the 'Conservative Prime Minister', (iii) the Labour government ministers who played a part in creating the National Health Service.
   b Did all the people you have identified play an equally important part in creating the Welfare State? Explain your answer.
3. Look back to pages 10–12. What did Lloyd George do between 1908 and 1912 to improve welfare provision?
4. Which of Sources 3, 4 and 5 do you think gives the best assessment of individuals' contributions to the Welfare State? Explain your answer.
5. Sources 3, 4 and 5 are taken from newspapers:
   a *The Daily Herald*, in which Source 3 appeared, supported the Labour Party. Griffiths and Bevan were Labour ministers. Might this have affected the way the cartoon portrayed the creation of the Welfare State?
   b *The Times*, from which Source 4 is taken, claimed that it did not support any political party. Might this have affected the view expressed in Source 4?
   c Source 5 comes from *The Observer*, at that time a Liberal newspaper. How might this have affected its point of view?
6. **a** Explain in your own words why Professor Pimlott suggests that the Welfare State was 'Hitler's revolution'.
   b Does this mean that Hitler can be considered as one of the people who created the Welfare State? Explain your answer.